JUMPING

Kate Needham
Designed by Ian McNee

Illustrated by Mikki Rain
Photographs by Kit Houghton
Consultant: Juliet Mander BHSII

Series Editor: Cheryl Evans

Contents

ALL ABOUT JUMPING

It may surprise you to know that horses and ponies are not natural jumpers. In the wild they only jump to escape from something, and most would opt to go around an obstacle if given the choice. It's fairly easy to train horses and ponies to jump, however and most enjoy it once they have learned.

NATURAL ABILITY AND CONFORMATION

Although all ponies are able to jump, some are naturally better at it than others. One of the things that influences a pony's natural jumping ability is his conformation, which means the shape and proportions of his body.

Jumping is a strenuous sport and a pony with good conformation is less likely to suffer strain or injury. His natural jumping style is also likely to be better, which should enable him to jump higher and with less effort than one with poor style.

The picture opposite shows some good points of conformation that can influence a pony's natural jumping style and ability.

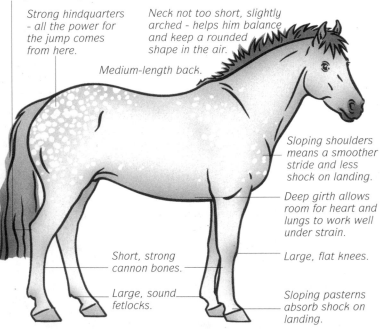

Large, sound hocks, free from any heat, lumps or swelling.

Well-proportioned forehand (head, neck, shoulders and front legs).

Strong hindquarters - all the power for the jump comes from here.

Neck not too short, slightly arched - helps him balance and keep a rounded shape in the air.

Medium-length back.

Sloping shoulders means a smoother stride and less shock on landing.

Deep girth allows room for heart and lungs to work well under strain.

Short, strong cannon bones.

Large, flat knees.

Large, sound fetlocks.

Sloping pasterns absorb shock on landing.

LEARNING TO JUMP

Jump training for pony or rider starts on the flat.

Poles on the ground are an introduction to jumps.

A variety of small jumps are introduced gradually.

When learning to jump, the training process is quite similar for pony and rider. However, an inexperienced rider should never try to learn with an equally inexperienced pony.

As with any training partnership, the beginner will learn from the more experienced. Confidence is essential to jumping and two beginners are likely to make each other nervous.

In order for pony or rider to gain confidence, it is important to progress steadily. This book shows some of the stages and exercises of early jump training.

TYPES OF JUMPING

Cross-country riders face a variety of formidable obstacles.

Once you know the basics of jumping there are many different types of fences and courses to specialize in. Show jumps are brightly painted fences set out in an enclosed arena. Top level show jumps are built to test how high and wide a horse can jump, but they will fall if knocked.

Cross-country jumps are solid obstacles set in the countryside with long stretches of gallop in between. A course of these fences requires lots of confidence and stamina from both the horse and the rider.

Steeplechase and point-to-point fences are designed to be taken at speed, and although you won't be encouraged to race over fences while learning, the basic technique is the same.

A top show jumper needs perfect style and precision to clear large fences cleanly and neatly.

Steeplechase and point-to-point races are restricted to adults but they are still fun to watch.

TACK AND EQUIPMENT

Jumping can be dangerous. You are often working at faster speeds, so if you do have a fall you are likely to fall harder. That's why it is doubly important to wear protective clothing and check all your equipment carefully. Make sure your tack fits well too, for comfort as well as safety reasons.

A PONY AND RIDER EQUIPPED FOR JUMPING

Crash hat with chin straps. It must meet current safety standards.

Gloves for protection and a better grip on the reins.

A bridle of reasonably thick leather. Showing bridles made of thin leather can easily break.

Riding boots with smooth soles, pointed toes and small heels.

A running martingale is often used for jumping. It stops the pony from lifting his head and getting out of control. Make sure it's correctly fitted (see below).

A body protector that meets current safety standards is essential for all jumping.

Long sleeved shirt or sweater.

Comfortable numnah, made of natural fibre such as cotton or sheepskin.

Forward-cut saddle (see below).

Jodhpurs or chaps.

Correctly fitting stainless steel stirrup irons.

Boots to protect legs.

Checking the fit of a running martingale

You should be able to fit a handspan between the rings and the withers.

Rubber stops prevent the rings slipping down to the bit.

Girth attachment

Different types of saddles

A jumping saddle is very forward-cut, specifically for use with shorter stirrups. It helps you keep a good position.

A general-purpose saddle is less forward-cut, but still fine for early jumping practice.

A straight-cut saddle, such as a dressage saddle, is designed for use with long stirrups and makes it hard to adopt a good jumping position.

Equipment checklist

- Check all stitching on the girth, stirrup leathers, reins and cheekpieces.
- Check all leather for cracks or signs of wear.
- Check the numnah is not pressing on the pony's spine, by pulling it up into the gullet of the saddle.
- Make sure any boots or bandages are correctly fitted and firmly fastened.
- Check the girth is done up tightly.
- Make sure the safety catches on the stirrup bars are down.
- Check that all tack and equipment fits correctly.

BOOTS

There are various types of boots, all designed to protect your pony's legs in some way. They must be put on correctly and fastened securely so that they do not come loose. Buckles fasten on the outside, pointing to the back.

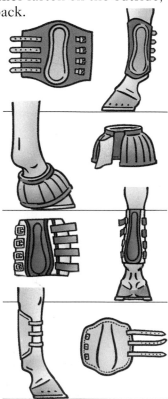

Brushing boots protect the legs from knocks and stop them from brushing against each other.

Over-reach boots protect the front heels from being trodden on by the back feet.

Tendon boots protect the back of the leg. They should fit the shape of your pony's leg.

Open-fronted tendon boots are useful for show jumping. They protect the tendons but a pony can still tell when he hits a pole.

BANDAGES

Exercise bandages protect the legs and give them some support. They are slightly elastic and must be put on correctly with even tension and padding such as Gamgee. They must be tight enough to stay firmly in place, but not so tight that they stop the blood in his legs. If you put them on yourself, make sure an experienced person checks your work.

Wrap Gamgee around the leg. Start bandaging just below the knee (or hock). Fold the loose end down and bandage over it as you go.

Loose end

Continue down the leg to the fetlock. Check each turn is of an even width and tension. Work back up towards the top, until you get to the tapes at the end of the bandage.

Tapes

Fasten these tapes and tuck under a fold. For extra safety, add plastic tape or sew over the fold. All tape must be no tighter than the rest of the bandage.

Plastic tape

STUDS

Studs are like small screws which are added to your pony's shoe to stop him from slipping. They are very useful on wet ground. The farrier includes special holes for them in your pony's shoes.

Thick studs are used for wet ground.

Smaller, pointed studs are for hard ground.

You will need an experienced person to help you put them in using a special stud key.

Studs are taken out after jumping and the holes filled with cotton wool coated with vaseline (or with special keepers).

Stud key

This part is used to restore the "thread" inside the stud hole.

This part is used to screw in studs.

This prevents them from getting packed with mud.

When not in use, keep studs in oil to stop them from getting rusty.

Stud holes are usually on the outside of each shoe.

ARE YOU READY TO JUMP?

Before you learn to jump you must have a secure riding seat, and be able to control your pony well in all three paces. Make sure that you can ride turns, circles and transitions confidently, and with balance, rhythm and impulsion. A warm up of at least twenty minutes is essential before any jumping session.

BALANCE, RHYTHM AND IMPULSION

These three words crop up over and over again in jumping lessons. Having your pony going forward with rhythm, impulsion and balance is the key to a good approach, and a good approach is the key to a good jump.

Balance means that you and your pony have your weight well distributed. If too much is on the forehand it will be harder to take off.

Rhythm means that the pace is steady and constant. On hard ground you may hear the regular hoof beat.

Impulsion means that your pony is moving forward willingly and easily, with lots of energy. His energy comes from his hind legs so they need to be beneath him, not trailing behind. He shouldn't be going too fast and must be under control.

Pony is unbalanced, with too much weight on his forehand.

Back is flat.

Hocks are trailing behind.

Nose is sticking out.

Mouth is resisting the bit.

Pony is well balanced, going forward with impulsion and rhythm in working trot.

Back is rounded.

Hocks are beneath him.

Rider has light rein contact.

Pony is accepting the bit and holding head correctly.

TRANSITIONS

Walk to trot   Trot to canter   Canter to trot   Trot to walk   Walk to halt

A transition is a change of pace, for example, from walk to trot or from walk to halt. Working on your transitions is the best way to improve the aids you use to tell your pony what to do and test his obedience. Practise changing pace at markers around the school. Start from walk to trot, then back to a walk and then halt. Eventually you can try from halt straight into trot.

IMPROVING YOUR BALANCE

A good way to improve your seat and balance is to work without stirrups or reins. You can practise without stirrups yourself but for work with no reins you need to be on a lunge (a long line that goes from a special noseband to an instructor in the middle of the school). The instructor controls the pony, while you concentrate on your position.

It may help to hold onto the pommel of the saddle at first when you trot. Relax your body and sit deep in the saddle to stop yourself from bouncing around.

If you are working without reins, knot them, so that they don't hang down.

If you are working without stirrups, cross them over the front of the saddle.

Arm exercises help you to relax your body and stay balanced. The girl here is twisting to each side with her arms held out to the sides.

TURNS AND CIRCLES

Work on turns and circles will improve your pony's suppleness. It's also good practice for his, and your, balance. Make sure you practise each way so that your pony does not become stiff on one side. If he does have a more supple side work this side first, then work the stiff side.

Start with large circles, using half the school. As your pony warms up try smaller ones. Use sitting trot for these. Figures of eight and serpentines work both sides in turn.

This pony is bending nicely around the rider's inside leg.

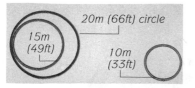

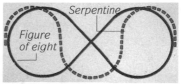

WARMING UP

* Walk on a long rein in both directions. Allow your pony to stretch out.
* Pick up contact with the reins and use your legs to tell your pony to start walking more actively.
* Practise transitions from walk to halt, then back to walk, and finally into trot.
* Establish an active working trot. Concentrate on getting him going with rhythm, balance and impulsion.
* Practise plenty of turns and circles on each rein, to get him bending correctly.
* Canter on each rein, making sure your pony is leading with the inside leg.
* Finish by walking quietly on a long rein and shorten your stirrups ready to jump.

YOUR POSITION

When jumping, it is important to make your pony's task as easy as possible. To do this you need to move your weight forward, off his back, in the position shown below. Shorter stirrups will help you keep your balance in this new position.

THE FORWARD POSITION

This picture shows you the correct position for jumping. Practise it at a standstill first. Then try it at a walk, trot and finally over trotting poles (see page 12).

Body folds forward from the hips, so that your weight is just off the pony's back. It should feel as if your stomach leads and your shoulders follow.

Head is up and looking straight ahead, between pony's ears. This helps keep your weight even, and lets you see where you are going.

Back should be straight, so that you bend from the hips not the waist.

Arms stretch forward to go with the pony's head.

Legs are more bent than in a normal riding position, which means shorter stirrups, see opposite.

Knees and ankles take all your weight and act as shock absorbers.

Lower legs remain straight and in contact with the pony's sides, so that you can still use them to give commands.

Heels point down. If your weight is in your toes, you will fall forward.

SHORTENING YOUR STIRRUPS

In the forward position, your weight is no longer in your seat. It goes through your knees and ankles to the stirrups, and you will find it easier to balance with shorter stirrups. Two holes shorter is usually about right, but try whatever feels comfortable for you. To shorten them while mounted, keep your feet in the stirrups and put the reins into one hand.

Take your leg away from the saddle and pull out the stirrup buckle with your free hand.

Pull the free end of the stirrup leather upward so that the pin of the buckle pops out.

Use your index finger to guide the pin into the new hole. Pull the leather back to its original position.

ALL ABOUT BALANCE

When you work your pony on the flat, his centre of gravity is through his girth, so you sit upright.

When jumping he has to balance on two feet, and his centre of gravity moves forward over his withers.

By using a forward position, you place your weight over his centre of gravity which helps him stay balanced.

COMMON MISTAKES

Bent waist and rounded back stops you going forward with the pony.

Tipping forward too much, too early puts weight on your pony's forehand, making it harder for him to take off.

Collapsing on landing is uncomfortable for your pony and means you're not ready for the next fence.

Lower legs back make your position insecure.

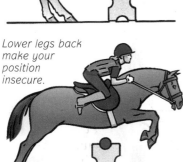

Looking down and leaning to one side unbalances your pony.

Getting left behind unbalances your pony and means you may pull on his mouth.

If your hands are fixed you will pull on your pony's mouth.

BEGINNER'S TIP

Neckstrap

A neckstrap is useful for novice riders with less than perfect balance. Hold onto it as you approach the fence to prevent yourself from accidentally pulling on your pony's mouth.

HOW A PONY JUMPS

Once you understand how a pony jumps, it's easier to see how you can help. You can learn a lot by watching top jumpers in action. They make sure that their horse or pony has a good straight approach, but interfere as little as possible while he actually jumps the fence. The jump can be broken down into the five phases shown below.

APPROACH

As the pony approaches the fence he sees it for the first time, so this is where the rider can be of most help. If the approach is straight and controlled, the pony has more time to study the fence he is about to jump.

The rider below is sitting slightly forward, but not too far in case she needs to sit down in the saddle and urge her pony on at the last moment. Her lower legs are straight, close to the pony's sides, and her hands are firm enough to keep the pony straight, but ready to move forward as he takes a good look at the fence.

Your pony's sight

Did you know that your pony has a blind spot? He can't see things immediately in front. This means that at the moment of takeoff, he cannot see the jump!

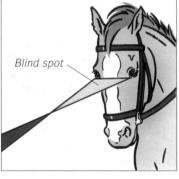

Blind spot

TAKEOFF

The pony bends his knees and lifts his front legs to take off. His neck arches which makes it look shorter, and his hindquarters come beneath him, ready for an upward spring.

The rider has let her hands move with his head, and as he lifts his shoulders, she folds farther forward from her hips, to take her weight off his back and stay in balance with him. If she did this too soon, she would make it harder for him to take off.

Rider bends forward from the hips, to remove weight from pony's back.

Hands have a light contact with the mouth, just enough to keep him straight.

Rider sits lightly in saddle, ready to urge him on.

Forelegs lift up.

Hind legs are underneath, ready to push off.

Pony stretches neck to look at fence.

IN THE AIR

All four feet are in the air, and the pony's head and neck are stretched right forward. His back has rounded into a nice curved shape which is called a "bascule" (see the diagrams on the right). His hind feet are stretched out behind, towards the point he took off from.

The rider has stayed still in the forward position, with her weight off his back. By looking ahead and keeping her lower leg straight, she is staying in balance with her pony.

See how the pony's neck goes right forward. This is why it's important to move your hands forward with the reins.

LANDING

The pony's forelegs stretch out to touch the ground, one at a time. He brings his head back up to help him balance and to minimize the shock on his forehand. His back legs are tucking neatly in behind. If they didn't he might catch the top of the fence.

The rider absorbs all the shock of landing through her ankles and knees. If she fell back into the saddle it would be uncomfortable for her pony and throw him off balance. Her hands are light so that she doesn't jab him in the mouth.

By looking ahead the rider keeps the pony straight, as well as seeing what's coming next.

GET-AWAY

As soon as his front feet touch down, the pony brings his back feet underneath him to take the weight off his forehand. Now he is ready to move into the first new stride.

The rider returns to her position for approach, and concentrates on a good rhythm, so that they are ready for the next fence.

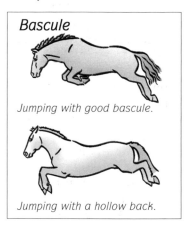

Bascule

Jumping with good bascule.

Jumping with a hollow back.

Hind legs tuck in underneath to clear fence and be ready to land.

Rider sits more upright. Her weight is in the stirrups, not the saddle.

This leg takes all the weight for a brief moment.

POLEWORK

Working over poles on the ground is an excellent introduction to jumping for you and your pony. It will give you both confidence, and improve your rhythm and balance. Ideally, you should practise all these exercises with an instructor who can help you correct your position as you work.

FIRST POLES

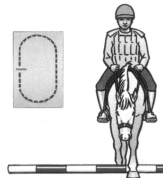

Start by placing a single pole on the ground, at the edge of the arena. Walk over it a couple of times in each direction. Let your hands move forward slightly as your pony stretches his neck.

Now try trotting over it. Concentrate on keeping a good rhythm and plenty of impulsion, so that your pony does not knock the pole. Add more poles around the arena, keeping them spaced well apart.

About the poles
- Use solid, rounded poles that will roll if the pony knocks them.
- They should be about 10cm (4in) thick and 3-3.5m (10-12ft) long.
- Paint them in bright stripes so that your pony can see them easily and get used to bright jumps.
- Have someone on the ground to help you move the poles around.
- Place them against a wall to help you keep straight and stop your pony from running out (see page 21).

TROTTING POLES

Raise alternate ends of each pole.

Place three poles in a row, with about 1.35m (4½ft) between each one. Get your pony going steadily at a rising trot, and then ride over the poles. Chanting, "one-two, one-two" as you go, may help your rhythm.

When your pony is trotting rhythmically over these, add an extra pole. Keep adding, until you have a line of six poles. To test your balance, try riding over them in your jumping position (see page 8).

For more advanced work, raise the poles slightly off the ground, to make your pony lift his knees and hocks higher. Place a low block or brick under alternate ends so that he trots over the middle.

Keep your pony going with impulsion and a good rhythm, so that he lifts his feet and avoids knocking the poles.

Tips for trotting poles

- Always look straight ahead to help you keep a straight course.
- Be careful not to jab your pony in the mouth. Use a neckstrap if necessary (see page 9).
- Don't overdo this work. Stop while your pony is doing well, and before he gets bored.
- Never use only two poles. Your pony may think he has to jump them.
- Make sure you ride over the poles from both directions, so that you work your pony on each side.
- Always ride exactly in the middle of the poles.
- If your pony gets over-excited, turn him in a large circle in front of the poles until he calms down.

HOW TO MEASURE DISTANCES

It's important to get the distances correct between trotting poles. In lessons your instructor will place the poles for you, but if you set up your own, you need to work it out for yourself.

To do this, count how many footsteps, placed heel to toe, fit between the poles set up for you in a lesson.

When you start jumping it is equally important to measure distances correctly. As they are longer, it is more useful to use strides.

All the distances given in this book are about right for a 14.2hh pony. Tables like the one on the right give approximate distances for smaller ponies.

Trotting pole distances	
Pony's height	Distance
12.2hh	1m (3½ft)
13.2hh	1.2m (4ft)
14.2hh	1.35m (4½ft)

Counting footsteps between poles.

Counting strides between jumps.

The correct distance always depends on your pony's size and length of stride.

If the distances are correct your pony should step in the middle, between the poles like this.

FIRST FENCES

Once you can trot confidently over a line of poles and keep a balanced jumping position, you should be ready to try your first fence. Start with a low cross pole. As you improve, try different types of fences, but always keep them low and never do too much in case your pony gets bored and misbehaves.

CROSS POLE

A low cross pole is the simplest fence to jump. The cross helps your pony aim for the centre. If you are with others, jump towards them, as your pony will be happier going towards his friends.

Approach at a steady trot initially, exactly as for the trotting poles. It can be helpful to use a placing pole at first (see below).

Reasons for a trot approach
• You have more control.
• You have more time to prepare for the jump.
• Your pony has more time to look at the jump.
• The trotting stride is shorter, so it's easier to reach the correct point for takeoff.
• A slower pace makes it easier to keep balance and rhythm.

USING A PLACING POLE

The placing pole helps you judge the distance to the jump.

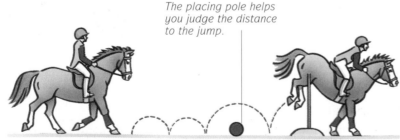

A placing pole will encourage your pony to take off at the right place, making the jump more comfortable for both of you. It should be placed about 2-2.7m (7-9ft) in front of the jump for a trotted approach.

Your pony will trot over the pole and then jump the cross. Make sure you do not jab him in the mouth as he takes off. Use a neckstrap (see page 9) if you find it difficult to balance.

You could also try jumping a cross pole after a line of trotting poles. It's good practice for you (it helps your balance and rhythm) and for your pony (it makes him more supple and improves his technique).

ALL ABOUT GROUND LINES

A pole placed in front of a fence, makes a clear ground line.

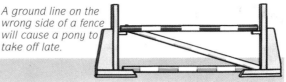

A ground line on the wrong side of a fence will cause a pony to take off late.

A pony judges a fence from the ground up, so the "ground line", which refers to the part of the fence which is nearest to the ground, is what he uses to judge when to take off. Ideally it should be slightly in front of the fence.

A false ground line is when the base of a fence is behind the front part. It is very confusing for a pony and will cause him to take off too late, knocking the fence or even falling. Avoid practising over fences like these.

JUMPING SPREAD FENCES

In a spread, one or more higher poles are added behind the first. Spreads usually slope upwards from the ground which means they can only be jumped one way. If jumped the wrong way, they give a false ground line (see above).

They may look bigger to you, but in fact their shape helps your pony to "bascule" as he jumps (see page 11).

JUMPING UPRIGHT FENCES

An upright fence is one where all the poles are set directly above one another.

It's quite hard for the pony, as he has to judge the height immediately and take off a suitable distance away to clear the fence. For this reason it is especially important to approach an upright fence straight, in

good control and with plenty of impulsion.

You can make an upright easier, by placing a pole on the ground slightly in front of the fence.

INTRODUCING GRIDS

Gridwork is a bit like polework, but with jumps instead of poles on the ground. It is a great way to build up confidence and introduce new jumps. The distance between jumps is important so that your pony gets the correct takeoff point each time, so it's best to practise with your instructor. She can set up all the jumps for you too.

BUILDING UP A GRID

Always build up your grid gradually, and make sure that you are comfortable at each stage before going on to the next. Keep the hardest jumps to the end.

Benefits of gridwork
- It improves your rhythm.
- It makes your pony more supple.
- It's good practice for your balance.
- It encourages you to jump in a straight line.
- It makes you practise a good position.
- It's an excellent way of building up confidence over low fences. You can make the last fence bigger, but always keep the first ones small.

Double cross pole

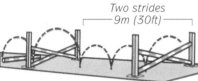

Two strides
9m (30ft)

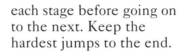

One stride
5.4m (18ft)

Start with a placing pole and two cross poles, about 9m (30ft) apart. Your pony will land over the first cross, take two strides and then take off for the second.

When ready, move the second cross pole closer (5.4m (18ft) from the first). This will allow your pony only one stride between the cross poles.

Treble cross pole

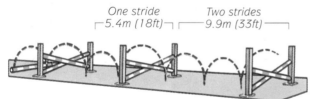

One stride
5.4m (18ft)

Two strides
9.9m (33ft)

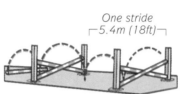

One stride
5.4m (18ft)

One stride
6.4m (21ft)

Add a third cross pole, two strides on from the second (9.9m (33ft)). Then close the gap to allow only one stride (6.4m (21ft)).

Note that with the third fence the distances increase slightly, as your pony will lengthen his stride as he jumps.

Varying the fences

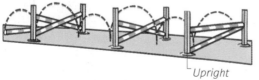

5.4m (18ft) *6.4m (21ft)*

Upright

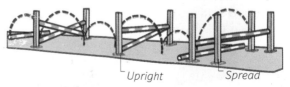

5.4m (18ft) *6.4m (21ft)*

Upright *Spread*

When you are confident over this, try varying the last fence. Raise one end of the last cross pole, to make an upright.

Then add a pole behind to make a spread. Finally change the second fence to an upright. Always have the biggest fence last.

BOUNCE FENCES

A bounce fence is when a pony jumps one fence and then takes off for the second one as soon as he lands, with no strides in between.

Practising over this type of fence is good for your pony's suppleness and for your balance. Make sure you have warmed up over a few easier fences first.

Start with two small cross poles about 3m (10ft) apart. Add on fences one at a time, increasing their distance apart by about 30cm (1ft) each time.

A grid including bounce fences is a good test of your balance and your pony's suppleness. Always build up gradually.

LEARNING ABOUT YOUR PONY'S STRIDE

For more advanced jumping you need to be able to judge the length of your pony's stride. Gridwork is a good chance to learn more about this.

When practising with a class of similar-sized ponies, compare to see whether yours has a short stride (does he have to stretch to make the second part of a double?) or a long stride (does he get too close to the second part?).

The distances in the table are for ponies with average strides, which is how fences are usually set up in a competition. If your pony's stride is short the fences may be too far apart; if long, they may be too close.

What influences a stride?
* Size – bigger ponies tend to have longer strides.
* Pace of approach – the faster it is, the longer his stride will be.

* Number of fences in a row – a pony needs more room as he progresses down a line.
* Ground conditions – if soft, the stride will be shorter.

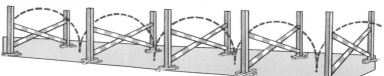

Approximate distances for grids approached in trot					
Pony's height	Placing pole to fence 1	Fence 1-2		Fence 2-3	
		2 strides	1 stride	2 strides	1 stride
12.2hh	2.1m (7 ft)	8.5m (28ft)	4.8m (16ft)	9.4m (31ft)	5.8m (19ft)
13.2hh	2.4m (8ft)	8.8m (29ft)	5.1m (17ft)	9.7m (32ft)	6m (20ft)
14.2hh	2.7m (9ft)	9m (30ft)	5.4m (18ft)	9.9m (33ft)	6.4m (21ft)

TOWARDS A COURSE

As your jumping improves, you can practise jumping several fences together from a canter. It's still essential to keep good impulsion, rhythm and balance and it's important to plan your route carefully so that your approach to each fence is straight. Once you can do all this, you'll be ready to tackle a complete course.

JUMPING FROM A CANTER

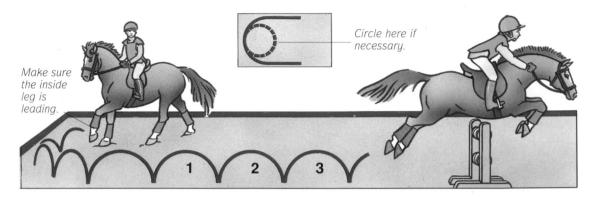

Circle here if necessary.

Make sure the inside leg is leading.

1 2 3

When jumping from a canter, make sure your pony is leading with the correct leg (the inside leg). Otherwise he will be off-balance. The best way to do this is to ask him to canter at a corner when he is bending the right way. If he is wrong, go forward into trot and circle until you get him going correctly.

Count out the last three strides into the fence. This will help you become familiar with your pony's stride. Practise this over a pole on the ground first.

CHANGING DIRECTION

When working at canter, you need to change the leg your pony leads with each time you change direction.

The easiest way to do this is to go forward into trot, then ask him to canter again once you have changed direction. This picture shows how to set up your jumps to practise this.

Have your pony cantering on the left leg for fence one. Go into trot at F and canter on the right leg just before or after A. Trot again after fence two and canter on the left leg just before or after C.

If necessary circle at A or C until your pony settles or strikes off on the correct leading leg.

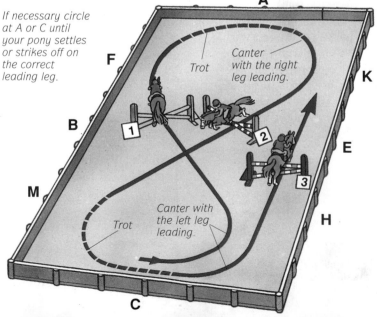

A

F

Trot

Canter with the right leg leading.

K

B

1

2

E

M

3

Canter with the left leg leading.

Trot

H

C

18

PRACTISING A STRAIGHT APPROACH

When you jump away from the sides of the school, it's harder to keep straight. You need to plan your approach carefully so that you don't turn into the jump too soon or too late.

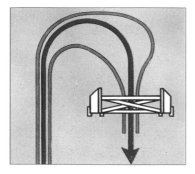

The red line shows a good approach. The blue lines show poor ones.

The key to a good straight approach is to keep looking ahead. This rider is already looking ahead to the fence as she turns into it.

PLANNING A GOOD ROUTE

Although it is helpful to turn a circle before a jump when schooling, it is not allowed in competitions.

You must plan a careful route with long, flowing turns that lead to a straight approach for each fence.

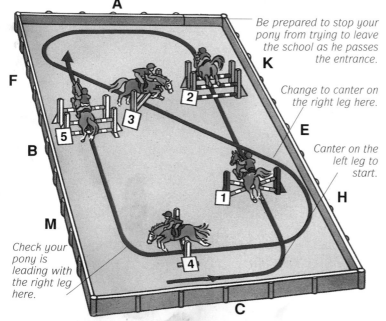

Be prepared to stop your pony from trying to leave the school as he passes the entrance.

Change to canter on the right leg here.

Canter on the left leg to start.

Check your pony is leading with the right leg here.

It's a good idea to walk the route yourself first on foot. Then ride through it with the poles on the ground.

This picture shows a well planned route over five jumps. The first two fences are in line and so fairly easy, but you must plan a careful approach to the third. Make a wide loop and don't let your pony cut the corner.

The best route to fence four is around fence one. If you cut in front of it, the turn will be sharp and you won't have time to change legs. Check your pony is still cantering on the right leg after fence four (some change legs as they jump). Don't race home over the last. Keep a steady, rhythmic pace.

WHEN THINGS GO WRONG

The most common reason for jumping mistakes is bad riding, but once a pony knows he can get away with something he is likely to continue being disobedient. Keep taking regular lessons so that your instructor can help sort out any problems straight away.

WHY PROBLEMS HAPPEN

Problem	Cause	Solution
He's afraid.	*The fence is too big.* *It's new and spooky.* *He hit it hard last time.* *He's had a bad fall.* *The ground is wet and slippery.*	*Go back to small fences.* *Follow another pony over.*
He's in pain.	*You are hurting him.* *His tack is uncomfortable.* *His feet or legs hurt - it could be that the ground is hard.*	*Ask your riding instructor for advice.* *Have a saddler check his tack.* *Ask the farrier to check his feet and legs and avoid jumping on hard ground.*
He's bored or tired.	*You've been jumping the same fences over and over again.* *He's unfit.*	*Take a break from jumping. When you start again do a little at a time and practise a variety of fences.*

RUSHING FENCES

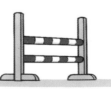

Rushing is when a pony suddenly speeds up as soon as he sees the jump. It can be that he's too eager, but it may also be that he's scared and wants to get over it as quickly as possible.

Build up his confidence over small fences, and try not to pull on the reins as this usually makes things worse. If you are tense, try to relax and concentrate on improving your rhythm.

Tips for correction
• Circle in front of the fence until he settles.
• Work over trotting poles and low grids to slow him down and improve rhythm.
• Approach in a walk, only breaking into trot a couple of strides before takeoff.
• Vary his work. Do a couple of jumps, then go out for a ride or school him on the flat.
• Keep the approach short.

KNOCKING DOWN FENCES

This is often caused by rushing, or a poor approach that leads to a poor takeoff.

If a rider catches the pony in the mouth on landing, the pony may pull his head up and drop his hind legs at the same time.

Pony takes off too late and catches pole with front legs.

Pony takes off too early and catches pole with back legs.

Tips for correction
- Concentrate on rhythm, balance and impulsion in the approach.
- Use bright poles and fillers (see page 22), to make him pay more attention to the jump.
- Practise over a variety of jumps, particularly spreads.
- Do plenty of gridwork.

REFUSALS AND RUNNING OUT

A refusal is when a pony stops dead and refuses to jump. Running out is when he runs to one side of the fence. If a pony starts to do either, find out why before it becomes a habit. Check all the things in the table on page 20 and ask your instructor for advice.

Tips for refusals
- Ride strongly into the jump, keeping both legs firmly against his sides.
- When he does jump, make sure that your hands move forward with his head.
- Follow another pony over.

Tips for running out
- Keep the approach slow but active and very straight.

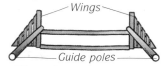

Wings

Guide poles

- Use wings on fences, and add guide poles to the sides of the jump.
- Place jumps against the side of the arena.

Beware of leaning forward too soon if your pony tends to stop. You may go over the fence without him!

- If he runs out to the right, make him turn back to the left, and vice versa. Try to stop him before he goes beyond the fence.

- Carry a whip. Have it on the side he runs out to.
- Keep fences wide – narrow ones are easier to run out at.

BUILDING JUMPS

If you want to build your own jumps to practise over at home, you'll need to collect a lot of good-quality equipment. Always build practice jumps in a safe place, and only use materials that won't damage your pony's legs if he hits them.

EQUIPMENT FOR SCHOOLING FENCES

Solid, round, wooden poles, as described on page 12, are best but they are heavy. Plastic ones are cheaper and lighter, and so easier to use at home.

Rustic poles   Painted poles

Cups fit onto a stand. Plastic ones are safest. Metal ones must never be left on the stand without poles, as they can cause injury.

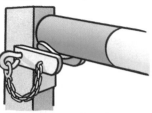

Cups are curved so that a pole will roll off, if knocked hard.

Stands must be solid, strong and stable. The best are the purpose-built wings which help frame a jump and discourage ponies from running out.

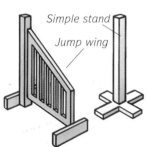

Simple stand

Jump wing

Plastic blocks can be used instead of wings and cups. They are light and can be stacked on top of each other easily to make different jumps.

BUILDING SCHOOLING FENCES

This fence looks flimsy and your pony will find it harder to jump.

Adding extra poles, a ground line and wings makes it more inviting.

Fillers like these, make a fence look more solid.

The best place to set up practice jumps is in an enclosed arena or a small field. It should be at least 20 x 40m (65 x 130ft), bigger for several jumps.

Make sure the ground conditions are good. Wet, slippery, hard or rutted ground may frighten a pony and can be dangerous.

If jumping in a field,

choose a flat, grassy area that is well-drained. Avoid jumping in the field your pony lives in, as it will ruin all his grass.

Try to make fences look as solid as possible by adding poles or special fillers. You can buy a variety of these or use things like bales or barrels as shown on page 23.

Safety checklist
- Build solid-looking jumps.
- Avoid flimsy materials.
- Include a ground line.
- Keep jumps wide.
- Check the ground on each side of the fence.
- Make sure there are no sharp edges.
- Keep all jumps in good condition and stack away neatly after use.

OTHER TYPES OF JUMPS TO BUILD

Tyres

Tyres threaded onto a pole make a well-shaped jump and won't hurt your pony's feet if he knocks them. Ask your local garage if they have any old ones that you could have.

Straw bales

Stack them up in various different ways and use extra ones to make wings. Make sure there is no loose string that your pony could catch a foot in. Remember to put them away at night if you intend to use them later.

Logs

Fallen trees can be excellent jumps. Make sure the ground is safe on either side before you jump, or arrange to have the trunk moved to a suitable spot. Ask an adult to saw off any sharp edges or branches that stick out.

Empty oil barrels

Only use barrels in good condition with no rust. Paint them if you like. If you use them on their sides, put pegs in the ground to stop them from rolling. When knocked, they make a loud noise which can scare a pony, so it's best to add a pole above them.

STORING JUMPS

Stack unused jump materials neatly in a fenced off area of the field or a spare shed. Never leave cups lying around.

SHOW JUMPING

Show jumping competitions take place in indoor or outdoor arenas. The jumps can be quite high, but they are built so that they fall if knocked hard. There are plenty of novice events organized by Riding and Pony Clubs that you can take part in, as well as the more professional ones.

WHICH CLASS TO ENTER?

Classes can be limited by the height of your pony (for example 13.2hh and under), by your age (for example under 14) or by experience.

Minimus classes are for ponies and riders who have never won anything, whereas an Open Class has no restrictions. Novice and Intermediate are somewhere in between. Don't be too ambitious, opt for an easy class to begin with.

Some shows have "Clear-round" classes which are excellent for beginners. Competitors ride the course once only and get a rosette if they jump clear.

Equitation jumping is also good practice. You are judged on style as well as a clear round.

This picture shows some of the common obstacles found in a show jumping ring. The red line indicates a shorter "jump-off" version of the same course (see right).

3. Spread fence with shark's teeth fillers – can be spooky.

4. Gate – an upright that is easily knocked as it hangs on flat cups.

5. Ornamental wall – looks solid but some ponies find it spooky.

6. Planks – these also hang on flat cups and fall easily.

7. Parallel bars – one of the hardest types of spread, as the front pole is as high as the back one.

Entrance from collecting ring – pony may try to turn home.

Take care here to be straight and change leading legs.

Go around fence 9.

2. Upright poles – looks quite airy so make a steady approach.

1. Brush with rustic poles – all natural materials, so not spooky.

8. Double including a spread (A) and a palisade(B).

9. Stile – narrow, so needs an accurate approach.

WALKING THE COURSE

Before your class starts you will be allowed into the arena on foot to take a closer look at the fences. Make sure you are smartly dressed. There is usually a map showing which order you jump the fences in, but they will also be numbered.

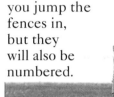

Decide on how best to approach each fence.

If there is time, watch the first few riders jump the course.

Note where problems occur and be ready for them.

Tips

* Walk the exact route you plan to ride.
* Work out where you need to change leading legs.
* By all means take a friend for advice, but don't get distracted.
* Check what the ground is like and look for any slight slope that may alter your pony's stride.
* Pace out the distances in any doubles or trebles.
* Look out for any spooky objects around the ring.

COMPETITION RULES

Most competitions have two rounds. In the first, the aim is to jump clear. For each mistake you make, you will usually get the penalty points listed below.

Competitors who go clear then jump a second round called the "jump-off". It's usually a shorter course of higher jumps and is often "against the clock". This means the fastest clear round wins.

Penalty points

* 3 for first refusal, run-out or circling in front of a fence.
* 4 for a knock-down.
* 6 for second refusal.
* 8 if you fall off.
* Elimination for third refusal, taking the wrong course, starting before the bell or failing to pass through the start or finish.

CROSS-COUNTRY

Most early jump training is done over schooling fences in a flat, enclosed arena. Cross-country jumps are set in the open across all kinds of different terrain. They are built from natural materials but include many natural obstacles which some ponies find as spooky as brightly painted poles.

JUMPING UPHILL AND DOWNHILL

Before you tackle jumps on a slope, practise trotting and cantering up and down gradually steeper hills. As a pony has four legs, it is easier for him to go directly up or down. If he zigzagged downhill, as we might, his hindquarters would swing out, overtake his front legs and throw him off-balance.

Going downhill is less effort for your pony but he will take longer strides and have more problems keeping his balance. When jumping downhill you need

Riding downhill needs good balance.

to approach slowly, in good control and balance. Don't lean too far forward. For more about downhill jumps, see the section on drop fences below.

Ponies need plenty of impulsion for uphill work.

Going uphill, he will take shorter strides and use lots of extra effort. If jumping uphill he needs lots of impulsion, so approach in a short bouncy canter.

DROP FENCES

By sitting slightly back on landing, you help your pony's balance.

Make sure you don't pull on his mouth as you land.

A drop fence is one where the ground on the landing side is lower than it is on the takeoff. Often this means that a pony cannot see where he will land and so has to trust you.

Try a small step down first. If necessary let him stand on top and look but don't let him turn away. Keep your leg on the girth and your body balanced.

Approach larger drop fences at a steady pace but keep the pressure of your legs against his sides. This encourages a longer stride, so that he jumps out well. Sit slightly back on landing.

WATER

Some ponies are terrified of water and will refuse to go near it. Others adore it, will splash around in it, and even try to roll. You may have a hard time getting them out again.

Try to introduce your pony to water while out on a ride. If necessary follow another pony in. Let him paddle and get used to it.

Once he is happy in water, try a small jump just after it. Let him take off from dry land at first. The water will slow him down, so you need to approach with plenty of impulsion.

Jumping down into water can be nerve-racking for your pony. He has no idea how deep it is. While building up his confidence, allow him to land on dry land first and then step into shallow water.

Water is one of the most difficult obstacles for some ponies.

TACKLING DITCHES

A natural ditch

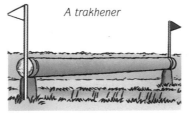

A trakhener

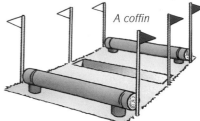

A coffin

Many ponies find ditches really frightening. To them, they look like a big black hole in the ground.

Try your pony over a small, natural ditch to start. You may come across one out riding, but make sure the ground is safe on both takeoff and landing sides.

If you sense your pony stopping as he spots the hole, squeeze with your lower leg to urge him on. Be ready for a large leap.

Two quite common cross-country jumps that include a ditch are a "trakhener", which is a ditch with a rail over it, and a "coffin", which has a ditch between two other fences. Approach the first part of a coffin slowly, so that your pony can see what's next. Keep lots of impulsion in case he hesitates in the middle.

RIDING A CROSS-COUNTRY COURSE

A cross-country course is spread out over several fields. The jumps are solid, with no top pole to fall off when knocked hard. For this reason they are only suitable for more experienced ponies and riders.

This picture shows some typical cross-country jumps. On a real course they would be spaced much farther apart than shown here.

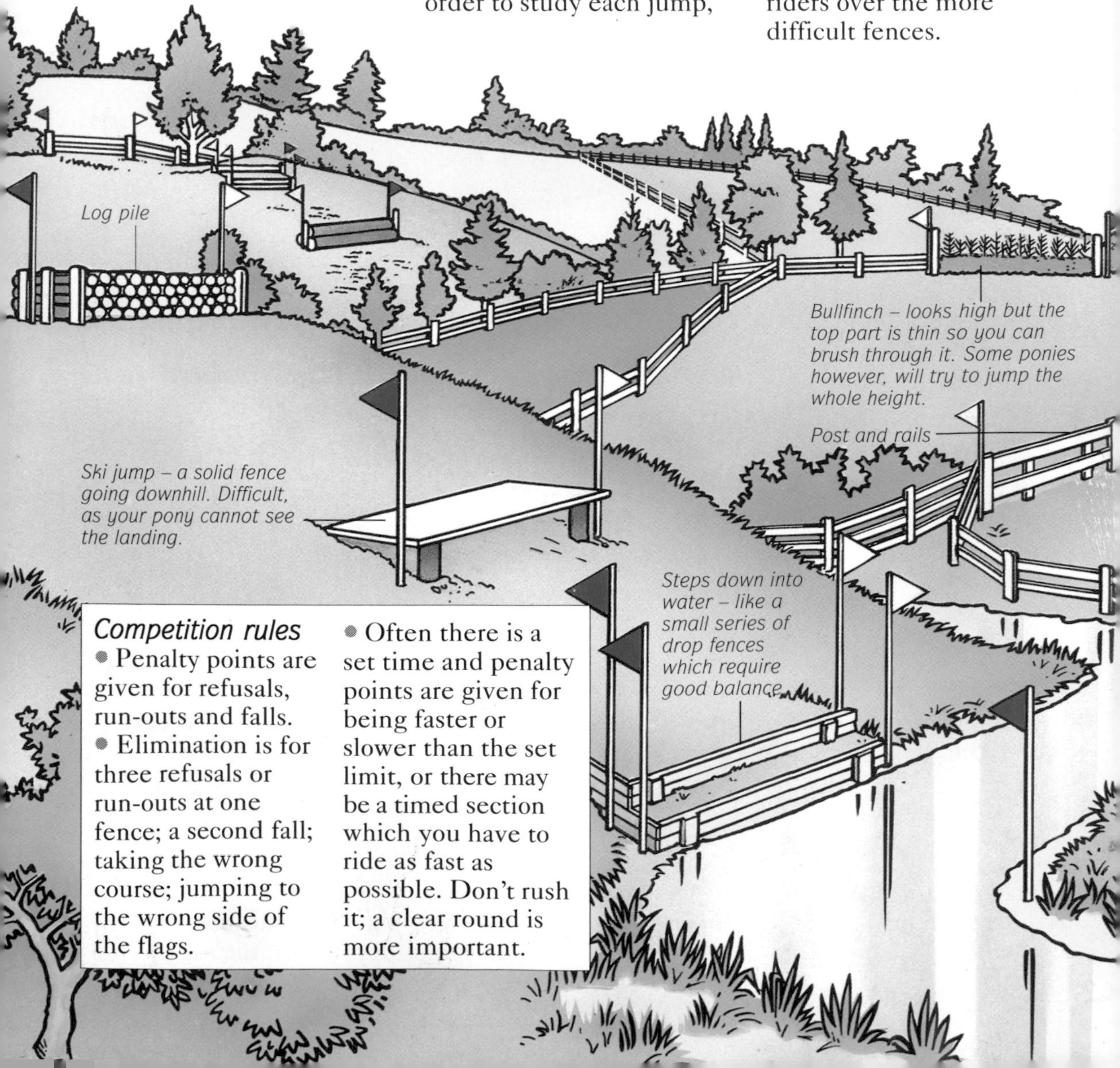

There are courses of varying standards around the country that you can arrange to practise over. Make sure you pick one of your level. Regular competitions are held over these courses too, as long as the ground conditions are good.

If competing, you need to walk the course first in order to study each jump,

plan your approach, and work out the correct route. This may take some time, but it is usually possible to visit the course the night before. The list on page 29 shows some of the things you need to consider.

If you are jumping late in your class, you may have time to go back onto the course and watch a few riders over the more difficult fences.

Log pile

Bullfinch – looks high but the top part is thin so you can brush through it. Some ponies however, will try to jump the whole height.

Post and rails

Ski jump – a solid fence going downhill. Difficult, as your pony cannot see the landing.

Steps down into water – like a small series of drop fences which require good balance.

Competition rules
- Penalty points are given for refusals, run-outs and falls.
- Elimination is for three refusals or run-outs at one fence; a second fall; taking the wrong course; jumping to the wrong side of the flags.
- Often there is a set time and penalty points are given for being faster or slower than the set limit, or there may be a timed section which you have to ride as fast as possible. Don't rush it; a clear round is more important.

Walking the course

* Check the ground conditions – are they soft or hard? If soft, takeoff and landing may get tricky for those jumping later.
* Plan your pace. Try and maintain a steady, balanced canter throughout the course so that your pony does not tire at the end.
* Think about the hills. An uphill section at the end will be tiring, so take the first part steadily.
* Some jumps may have several options. Consider which route your pony would jump best.
* Slow down to a trot in wooded sections with narrow, twisting paths.

Watch out for jumps into and out of woods or shaded areas. The change in light conditions will make it harder for your pony to see the fence well.

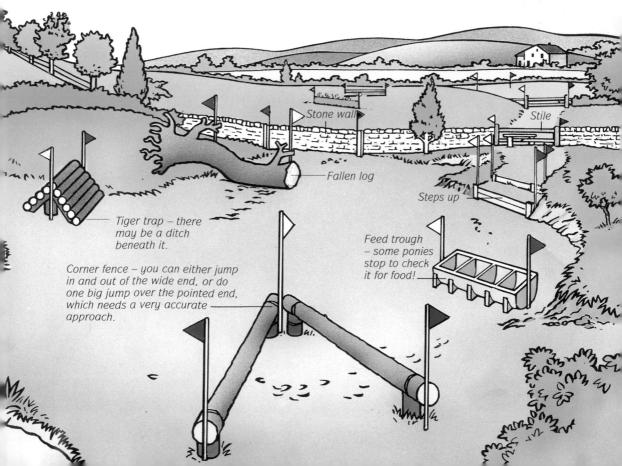

Stone wall

Stile

Fallen log

Steps up

Tiger trap – there may be a ditch beneath it.

Corner fence – you can either jump in and out of the wide end, or do one big jump over the pointed end, which needs a very accurate approach.

Feed trough – some ponies stop to check it for food!

OTHER EVENTS

Whether you are aiming for the top competitions or simply enjoy jumping for fun, you'll find a great variety of events to take part in. Keep watching too. You can learn a lot from the top riders, whether you see them on television or at a national show.

ONE, TWO, AND THREE-DAY EVENTS

These competitions consist of three separate sections: dressage, cross-country and show jumping. They test a horse and rider's all-round skills and stamina.

At Pony and Riding Club level, the event lasts one day. The dressage is a memorized test, where you are judged on performance, style and obedience. Your score is given as penalty points (so the lower it is, the better) and is added to your jumping scores.

The cross-country course must be completed clear, and within a set time to avoid penalty points. In the show jumping your aim is to jump clear too, as there is no jump-off. At the end

The cross-country course tests stamina and courage.

of the day the pony and rider with the fewest penalty points win.

More experienced riders and horses take part in two- and three-day events, which have two extra sections before the cross-country:

the roads and tracks, and the steeplechase. The roads and tracks section does not include jumps, but it does test the horse's stamina. The steeplechase is a course of brush fences which has to be ridden at speed.

Show jumping tests accuracy and ability.

Dressage tests obedience.

TEAM EVENTS

Both cross-country and show jumping events often include pairs classes. In show jumping, one pony and rider jump first and then hand a baton to the second pony and rider at the end of their round.

In cross-country, the two ponies and riders go around the course together. You can choose who gives the other a lead over most fences, but there may be a few where you are meant to jump side by side.

Wear the same colours to look smart as a pair.

In "team chase", an experienced horse can lead a novice over the fence.

Pairs classes are a good chance for a young pony to gain confidence from a more experienced one.

Team chasing is an exciting event which is usually only for senior riders. A team of four riders and horses follow each other around a cross-country course. The scores of the first three riders home are usually the ones counted.

NOVELTY CLASSES

Shows often have novelty events that you can take part in for fun, such as Chase-me-Charlie or Horse and Hound. You can usually enter on the day, so wait to see how tired your pony is from other classes first.

In Horse and Hound, you jump with your pony first and then do a second round with your dog! (See right.)

In Chase-me-Charlie, ponies and riders take turns jumping just one fence which is gradually raised higher and higher. You drop out once you knock it down or have a refusal.

The adult version of this is called the "Puissance", and usually includes three jumps of up to 1.8m (6ft) or more.

31

INDEX

With thanks to Claire Davies and Lady, Aimee Felus and Yogi, Claire Foreman and Tiggy, Tarn Hollands and Lela, Kerry Mason and Bobby, Charlotte Read and Fionnula, and the Horse Unit at Writtle Agricultural College.

First published in 1996 by Usborne Publishing Ltd, 83-85 Saffron Hill, London EC1N 8RT, England.

THE USBORNE RIDING SCHOOL